Myths from Which We Got Our Name

New Women's Voices Series, No. 167

poems by

Courtney Tala

Finishing Line Press
Georgetown, Kentucky

Myths from Which We Got Our Name

Copyright © 2022 by Courtney Tala
ISBN 979-8-88838-043-7 First Edition
All rights reserved under International and Pan-American Copyright Conventions. No part of this book may be reproduced in any manner whatsoever without written permission from the publisher, except in the case of brief quotations embodied in critical articles and reviews.

ACKNOWLEDGMENTS

Many thanks to the editors and readers of the following journals, in which these poems appear, sometimes in different forms:

Academy of American Poets/Poets.org: "There is a small TV mounted in the cobwebbed corner of the breakroom" and "Etymology of Your Name"
Glassworks Magazine: "all the texts i couldn't send after your third miscarriage"

Publisher: Leah Huete de Maines
Editor: Christen Kincaid
Cover Art: Lew Jeane Dizon
Author Photo: Mia Rae Photography
Cover Design: Elizabeth Maines McCleavy

Order online: www.finishinglinepress.com
also available on amazon.com

Author inquiries and mail orders:
Finishing Line Press
PO Box 1626
Georgetown, Kentucky 40324
USA

Table of Contents

Inheritance of Rage, or Tala Empathizes with her Father 1

Bedtime Story for My Possible Future Child 3

Examination of Grief, Ending with a Burning Cigarette 4

There is a small TV mounted in the cobwebbed corner of the breakroom 5

Etymology of Your Name 6

Punnett Square with Imagined Inheritance 7

For My Friend, In Reply to Your Question 8

all the texts i couldn't send after your third miscarriage 10

Punnett Square for Infertility 11

Like Palms in Prayer 12

Elegy for Mister Miyagi 13

In These Myths, the Mother Has No Name 15

The Mother Answers What the Historians Could Not 17

Gregor Mendel's Theory of Heredity 19

In the Church, My Best Friend's Father Wilts 20

At Dinner, the Waitress Mistakes My Best Friend for My Lover . 21

Reverse Miscarriage 22

On Being Asked to Elaborate on What I Mean by Trust 23

Lineage 25

Family Story Ending with an Impossible Promise 30

With Thanks 32

*"Look at the stars
Look how they shine for you"*
Chris Martin

"in order to contemplate lineage / you start with what you know"
Franny Choi

Inheritance of Rage, or Tala Empathizes with her Father

> *In Philippine mythology, Tala was the creator of the constellations. Her father, Bathala, creator of man and Earth. Compassionate yet volatile, he used storms, famine, or floods to punish transgressors. One day he left his kingdom and went into a deep slumber, never to return.*

How quiet the sky has become now, unbothered
by your fury. It's true, sometimes I miss

you, Father, but I know you left before
your anger could destroy us all.

When distant thunder rumbles, I'm reminded
of your voice. When the wind blows, I'm back

atop your shoulders, looking out over the kingdom
you built us in your name. What a shame

you aren't here to see it now. Each night
I toss a few more stars into the sky

and watch them as they smolder. By my hand
they rearrange, shifting in and out of place,

a glowing puzzle I've yet to solve.
When I saw the first star die,

burnt out in a brilliant supernova, I envied
its collapse. On Earth, people call this

beauty: a fleeting
flash, then the nothingness of night.

Sometimes, I feel my temper rise
like lightning through my veins

and in these moments, I'm sure I am
your daughter. I mold another orb of light

in my palms and think how easy it would be
to walk away and never look back. How easily

I could burn this all to the ground.

Bedtime Story for My Possible Future Child

If I should have a child, I imagine they'll want some light to soften the darkness of their room. Like my parents did for me, I'll build the universe into their ceiling, pressing each adhesive star into place one by one until the whole room glows. Many say the stars we see are already dead, but that's not quite right. Like us, they are born, they live. In the end, the light will go out. Darkness is not the opposite of light, just the absence of it. Praise the science for its small comfort, that even if something disappears it can somehow return. If my child fears the dark I'll tell them their mother is a descendant of the stars, sent to Earth from Tala herself. The story goes like this: Each shimmering orb, light-years away, is a cousin, a sibling. Each fractured constellation a limb branching from the same family tree. I'll tell them one day, when I'm gone, if they miss me, just look up. Light is the fastest thing in the universe. The stars burn far longer than our eyes will live to see.

Examination of Grief, Ending with a Burning Cigarette

No amount of wishful thinking can unmake a ghost.
    In the hospital, I held his hand. It withered
        as the flatline sliced the room. My family said

he waited for me. I wish they hadn't. I thought myself
    responsible. If I didn't come to see him,
        he would've woken up, gone back

to chain smoking on Grandma's front porch,
    rocking in the window recliner.
        Trace my bloodline backwards: it will not flow

to him, but still he was the grandpa I grew up with.
    He loved my grandma. That much
        we had in common. In that hospital I saw her

outlive love a second time. In his obituary,
    our names line up beside hers
        to form a list of those he left behind.

How painful this surviving: to live
    with the memory of his leaving. I can't forget
        the sound, a rush of breath gasping through his lips

before the stagnant air stilled.
    Shame on the mind for how it steeps in old pain,
        how it clings to what we want to forget. Already

I can't remember his voice, his cologne, his brand of cigarettes.
    I'm afraid that even with the strongest scents,
        such disappearing is inevitable. We remember

in fragments, a trigger shocking the brain
    into mourning. Even now sometimes I swear
        I hear his laugh. I see his face each time I smell smoke.

There is a small TV mounted in the cobwebbed corner of the breakroom

that is permanently set to the news & today the news is talking about an active shooter incident from this morning & the breakroom is intrigued, because it happened at the Navy base right down the street & now, after the shooter is confirmed dead & the victim is in the hospital, the news is calling it *an isolated domestic dispute* & in this case, *victim* is just another word for girlfriend of a man with a hot temper & a coworker peels his eyes from the screen & says to the room *guess she should've watched who she pissed off, huh?* & I fail to find the humor in the situation so I look for it in the bottom of my sad Tupperware while around me, the table erupts in a fit of corporate laughter & I would like to tell my coworker where he can stick his humor, but by now I have learned that *never* is the right time to open my mouth when I am the only woman in the room & it's been months, but I still remember my downstairs neighbor's voice as she screamed over her angry boyfriend & the sound of shattering glass that came next, then the silence, pierced by the front door slam & when I stepped outside later, all I could see was blood, quietly dripping down the vinyl siding to pool on the landing outside their door & I thought *it's none of my business* as I called maintenance & asked them to clean the stairs & my coworkers are still chuckling when the TV shows a clip of a reporter standing outside Oceana, who says the victim is *lucky & in stable condition*, which really means her ex-boyfriend emptied five bullets into her & just had bad aim & the news plays on a continuous loop, so it tells us again that an incident happened just under six miles from here, which is to say danger is lurking just around the corner, or maybe just downstairs & my coworkers have finished their lunches now & someone clicks off the TV.

Etymology of Your Name

after Martín Espada
for Mila

Huddled together in the hospital waiting room,
nine of us share five chairs. In the maternity ward,
a tone chimes through a speaker to signal each new birth,
and we wonder which one marks
the inception of your life. You, an impossible
embryo that made it full-term.

The prefix *in-* means *negative*, as in the minus sign
forming on each plastic test, and when paired with its root word
fertilis, it became something too much to bear.
So none of us spoke, just spent years holding our breath.
But now, somewhere a song floats over our heads and the doors
swing open, revealing your father, eyes wild and weary,

his arms raised in victory. The entire room
breathes and the tension in your grandma's neck
unwinds. Your grandpa grabs her hand, his eyes looking
to the ceiling to make space for what is welling
and we celebrate, a jubilant tangle of limbs.

You do not know that three were lost before you,
or that two more were lost since.
You do not know that no more will come after,
that *only* will become a word to you as familiar as home.
You don't know yet that *milagro* means *miracle*,
just that Mila is your name, and we sing it, an off-key chorus
filling the room with its sound.

Punnett Square with Imagined Inheritance

When we speak of origins, how far back should we go? What pieces will we omit if our future kids come wondering how we met? Make no mention of the alcohol, how we had too much and spent the evening laughing in someone's tiny kitchen. Tell them, instead, how I woke, your name, a lyric buzzing in my throat. Or start days later, tell them of that night by the fire at a bar that maybe won't exist by then. Of the flames and smoke that burned our eyes, of the fever in our blood.	When the fever comes, we laugh, for now is not the time for children. Even still, some nights we lie awake and build them in our heads, connect the dots to form our perfect image. Half the fun is in the trying, a game we play to predict which fragments of us will emerge in them. Our heads fill with this imagined inheritance, of two kids with only the best traits we have to offer. We try to guess if they'll look more like him or me though we know their appearance is left entirely to chance.
Say originate. Say inherit. Say fade. So intertwined that one can't be mentioned without thinking of the others. How much of my history was lost before it made its way to me? There's so much to hold onto, family stories I swore I'd never forget yet struggle to remember. I'd burn all my useless memories just to make room for those, to save these shards and build a path so one day, my children, and all that come after, can trace their blood to where it starts.	There is a chance they'll look like me, but I know the odds are against me. We've crossed our genes. We've watched them fade away. For our possible child, I fear we'll find no dolls that look like them, no fairytales or superheroes they can see themselves becoming. That they'll feel the way I did, reaching for a heritage slipping from their grasp. So I'll tell them stories of home, of Heaven, the myths from which we got our name. Of stars, the traces they'll find inside their blood.

For My Friend, In Reply to Your Question

after RA Villanueva

I'd like to say good,
but I'd rather not
lie. Instead, I'll say *Just tired*,
which is at least half
true. I won't mention
another month passing
with no blood, how I'm trying
not to blame my faulty body.
Won't mention the tests
and appointments, needle pricks
and draws, the vials—
filled with what I should
but do not shed. Instead,
let me ask you of the last time
we spoke. You mentioned
the story of a killer whale,
how she carried her still-
born calf for seventeen
days. Scientists called it
record-setting, assumed she'd lost
at least two others before showing
this unusual display
of grief. How backwards,
to marvel at this parade
of mourning.
Did you see that now,
almost two years later,
she's pregnant again?
I want to believe in miracles,
but it seems the numbers
are against us. The whales,
endangered, are desperate
for any live birth. Scientists say
less than half are a success.

With those odds it's hard
to hope. They say for every ten
meters you go beneath the ocean,
pressure increases by one
atmosphere. I wonder if she feels it
too, like the weight
of all the dead she's carried
piling up on her back.

all the texts i couldn't send after your third miscarriage

1. dilate? or evacuate?
   is there a word that means losing
   that which you've tried so hard to create?

2. that grainy black and white picture
   now just looks like static

3. the word apology—synonymous with
   red. with blood, fresh and harsh
   against the white porcelain bowl

4. your body, swollen
   but fruitless. beautiful,
   even when empty

5. and you, a hollowed pear,
   insides cut up by each
   slash of the minus sign

6. when i called after the first time
   and the second, i just couldn't speak
   her back into your body

7. this is the way we always love each other—
   with tight lips,
   and empty hands

Punnett Square for Infertility

When it comes to time it seems there's never enough. Curse the clock for how it erodes our biology, reducing all to dust. My cousin warns me not to wait, hopes I don't share her problems, but I fear our unfortunate genetics. Both our mothers struggled too, the reason why we're only children. Loved, but lonely, longing for a sibling or two to call our own. My body fills with nothing but uncertainty. So, I wait and wonder how much suffering we both inherited.	How much suffering did I inherit? My parents tried for years, test after test with nothing but one lonely line slashing through their desire for children. It wasn't until after they'd given up that the signs finally changed. Funny, how sometimes it seems God decides to withhold His blessings until we throw up our hands in defeat. It's almost as if we need to struggle, to reject Him, before God returns, demanding we believe.
When or if it comes, only time will tell. My doctor moves a wand inside me and points to the screen, calls my uterus *heart-shaped* then tells of my increased chance of miscarrying. It seems sometimes, that even when built with the best intentions, a home may not be suitable. My body, now a condemned house, cracks in the foundation fully on display. My love and I leave the appointment unsure of what it all means, what awaits us when we try.	I'll admit I did not believe in God or even miracles until I saw my cousin's child, born even after the doctors' diagnosis. Deemed impossible, yet now a second child forms in her. Oh, the sweet victory of overcome odds. How mysterious, the science of the body. How it changes all the rules without warning. Tell me, should this give me faith, or make me worry? I'm undecided, still unsure. Trying for patience as we see what awaits.

Like Palms in Prayer

Two weeks after the speculum is removed,
my doctor calls with news

of my traitorous cells, the urgent testing I now need.
Precancer, she calls it, and in that moment I'm afraid

of my own body, the cells that have possibly shed
the prefix already. When I hang up, I do not

pray. Maybe I've forgotten how. Instead I collapse,
the what-ifs playing a horrific loop in my mind.

When my love comes home, I consider keeping
the news a secret. My irrational fear: the cancer

will become fact the moment I reveal its possibility
to anyone other than myself. When I finally speak,

he kneels by the couch where I sit, limbs
carefully tucked, and we bow our heads. Again

we do not pray. My mouth finds
his with the urgency

of an unanswered question and he leads me
to bed, clothes falling from our bodies like

grace as we go. Every cell in my body,
an uncertainty, but of these things I'm sure.

His hand weaving through my hair— a promise
we'll hold onto. His breath mixing with mine,

the gentlest Amen. Our bodies
pressed together like palms in prayer,

a gospel in this godless bed.

Elegy for Mister Miyagi

Whenever we watch *The Karate Kid*
my mom thinks of her dad. She swears
they look exactly alike, but I don't see it.
the pictures hanging in the hall at Grandma's
look nothing like Mister Miyagi but she says
You just had to know him,
to which I have no retort.
I was born nine months too late,
missed the funeral and any chance
at knowing. Now I all I have are stories
of a time when I was nothing
more than the wishful air
blowing out a birthday candle.

My parents found out
they were pregnant sometime after the last
shovel of dirt was packed onto his grave.
I've always been on my own timing, showing up
after the doctors had given up hope.
I get my stubbornness from him, never
accepting when someone tells me no.
I can't tell you how many times
I watched *The Karate Kid* as a child,
but each time was like meeting my granddad.
We'd watch him teach *wax on, wax off*

and my mom would say
He laughed just like that, then whisper
I miss him as the scene ended.
I still don't see the resemblance, but I let it go.
Don't we search for our dead
in whoever we can feast our starving eyes on?
When we heard the actor who played him
died, my mother lost her father all over. Again,
we watched the movie, in silence this time,
and when the credits started we let them roll,

watching his name rise
then disappear, a procession
scrolling across our screen.

In These Myths, the Mother Has No Name

> *Bathala had three children with a mortal woman: Mayari,*
> *goddess of the moon, Hanan, goddess of the morning, and Tala,*
> *goddess of the stars.*

Perhaps the historians made an honest mistake.
Perhaps it was just clumsy editing,
no one realizing this mortal woman's name
didn't appear even once as the tales scrawled on,
these epics describing creation
of the Earth, of the heavens that held
Bathala and all his children.
In one story, the mother
died in childbirth, leaving
behind three baby girls, demigods
that Bathala carried home to the sky. They lived
with him in Heaven, watched him rule
as they grew from babies into women.
Did they call him God, or Father?
Did he tell stories of their mother,
or was her death seen
as weakness? Mortality, a trait
he ignored in hopes that they'd inherit only
the strongest parts of both of them.

In a different story, she lived.
He took to Heaven with the children, leaving her
on Earth with nothing
but distrust in any man who called himself
holy. By definition, a demigod is only half
divine, lesser than those pure gods
inhabiting the skies. The children grew up
feeling incomplete, as if a piece of them was tethered
to a place they couldn't name. At night,
they'd dream of distant places, their feet
touching down on solid ground to run towards

a point they couldn't remember when the first
sister woke. So a cycle began. The morning sun
sinking down beneath the horizon for the moon
to take its place. In the moon's dying light
a whisper of stars, falling
to catch a glimpse of the world below.

The Mother Answers What the Historians Could Not

Here I am, very much alive and ready
to put that story to bed. I didn't die
in childbirth. I pushed each screaming

goddess from my body then nursed
them off to sleep. Of course
history would try to make a martyr

of me, paint me as some nameless
thing unworthy of mention. Don't forget
I made those children. Half-

divine or not, something sacred formed inside
me. On Earth, I'm known as the holiest
one night stand. Their father used my body

as reliquary then left me here to watch him
gloat in the sky. I know he was God. I know
he made both Heaven and Earth, but every time

I hear a storm I curse that moody bastard.
I've seen his temper. Felt his strength.
When the sky roars with thunder I still feel

his breath against my neck.
What a fool I was to think his words
were anything more than rehearsed sermon.

He pillowtalked divine promises,
told me stories of his home in the sky.
How he'd take me there. Show me off.

He thought since he was God he could break
all his rules, but a mortal couldn't travel
home with him. Mad, embarrassed, he

ghosted. Gone before morning and just a note
that said *I'm sorry*. When he found out I was pregnant,
he snuck back down to take our daughters

back with him. Made some lie about my death
so he didn't have to speak of what he did. But I knew.
I feel his regret in every restless sky.

Gregor Mendel's Theory of Heredity

Mix two things together and it's inevitable
one trait will fade. In any hybrid one side is bound
to overcome the other. There's a formula
to this disappearance, the dilution of phenotypes
tied to the end of an equation.
It's simple, really. Each new generation a burial
of traits not strong enough to survive.
In another world, my older siblings
made it all the way to birth and none of them
looked like me. Maybe curly hair, or darker skin,
or eyes a shade more like our parents'.
Consider, for a moment, the resilience of the living.
How the genetic code trickling
through a bloodline is made entirely
of chance. By definition,
I was an unlikely outcome.
My existence and all its recessiveness
a surprise. Each masked trait, another gene
drowning in a forgotten pool
only to resurface years later, like an heirloom
we thought was lost forever but was really
right in front of us the entire time.

In the Church, My Best Friend's Father Wilts

His head: a half-wished-on dandelion. Thinning
gray hair drooping into his hands. No breeze

to feather through the strands. His wife neatly
folded in the casket beside us. My best friend says *We spent*

all night looking through old pictures. Remember the magnolias?
And how could I forget? Every memory I have begins

looking out my front door to the house that will always be
his. His mom, tending the tree in their front yard. One day

we climbed the tree, our clumsy feet knocking blossoms
to the ground. For a moment we sat, heads cradled in the canopy,

soothed by the explosion of perfume from each velvet bloom.
Beneath us, the ground littered with bulbs like discarded grenades,

the tattered petals crackling under our weight. When his mother saw,
she scolded us to stay out of her tree. We ran off to play

away from her watchful eyes. How careless we were
with such beauty, to not cherish while it was intact.

At Dinner the Waitress Mistakes My Best Friend for My Lover

for Lennore

Across from me, my best friend ordered
some fancy meal whose name neither of us
could pronounce. I laughed as she struggled,
the words a clumsy tangle spilling off her tongue.
She swatted my hand, rolled her eyes, but smirked
as I turned to order for myself. The waitress smiled
and left us, returning only to deliver our plates.
I remember when she tried her first bite,
how she closed her eyes as if to shut out
all sensation—the whining child beside us,
the obnoxious party of ten—other than taste.
How she insisted, *You have to try this*, then loaded
a bite onto her fork. How I leaned forward
to meet her at the center of the table and took
the small offering gently into my mouth. Funny
how something tastes better when given
from someone else's hand. And maybe this too is love,
to offer up small morsels in the hopes
that joy will spread across a beloved's face, a smear
of happiness starting at the corner of her mouth.
Praise these slivers of shared joy. Praise these gestures,
often unnoticed, but to anyone else
would look a lot like love.

Reverse Miscarriage

The blood picks itself up off the floor and trickles
back into your body. Back inside your body, each drop

soothes your stomach until your body is racked with
relief that washes over you, expelling

the anxiety engulfing your mind. You breathe,
inhaling the fear from the room until the air

is clean. You smile, knowing the flutter, whether real or imagined,
was felt. Science says there's an explanation for everything,

even this, woven into a chromosome you have
no control over. It's normal to feel nothing, then everything

all at once, trying to comprehend this process. Inside you,
your cells divide, pull apart into nothing at all.

On Being Asked to Elaborate on What I Mean by Trust

I will tell you of his arms
extended high above his head,

of standing, one foot in his hands,
the other stretched behind me

in a perfect arabesque.
I was taught that any stunt

is more likely to crumble
if the flyer thinks too hard, so there I was,

thoughtless, on display, concerned
only with performing for the crowd.

Tossed up in the air, his palms
became the only ground I had to stand on.

If he wobbled beneath me, I was told
to do nothing, to let him do all the work

of saving. Taught to never quit a stunt, I'd fight
until my base collapsed, and even then, I was told

to keep smiling. *Never let them know
you're falling.* We painted on our grins

though we knew the ground was rushing
up to crash against us. How many times

did my body hit the ground instead of landing
in his arms? How many times did I brace

myself for certain impact before
he reached in at the last second

and snatched me from the air?
If I hit the ground I risked a break,

a sprain, a certain ache. Even a clean catch
still left marks. Days after I would find

bruises in the shape of his fingerprints purpling
on my skin, faint reminders of his touch.

Lineage

According to myth, the gods
control the stars. Some nights
glow brighter than others. Picture
a dimmer, a switch the gods take turns
sliding to whatever brightness
fits their mood. Rationing
out their brilliance to the world
below. Or, picture the stars
as souls: our dead shining,
powering their lights towards home.
Always reaching for us
yet we see them only in darkness.
Come morning, how the light
fades: a fleeting, ghostly whisper.

//

Fleeting, like the whispers of ghosts,
our memories become unreliable at best.
They disappear if not recorded, or else
reappear cloaked in only shreds of truth.
How much of ourselves get lost with time?
Fragments lie forgotten beneath the cortex
of our brains, collecting dust. A thing
buried so long becomes impossible
to unearth. I pray for excavation, to be
both rememberer and the remembered.
That my children's children and those after
can build their own versions of me
once I'm gone, using
only what they've been told.

//

All I have is what I've been told.
What I know is this: Celestial
is my mother's surname, tying her
family's bodies to heaven. Granddad
was the first to go,
called home to wait for the next of us
to join him. Legend has it
that each soul has its own companion
star that it returns to in death. I wonder
if it's lonely, if he tires of sitting in the dark
and passes time by counting other specks
of distant light. I want to think otherwise.
That each time I see the flash of a shooting
star, it's really him, laughing.

//

There's a story of Granddad laughing
when he met my dad for the first time, back
when he was only boyfriend, not yet
husband or father. Granddad saw
my dad's last name and immediately knew
its meaning in Tagalog. *Your name
might mean star,* he said. *But don't forget
I'm Heavenly.* I imagine this joke: not a warning,
but approval. Grandad's way of accepting
that he would always be her sky, her heaven,
but at least my dad could be the light that brought her
home. That with his blessing and God's she'd become
part of a new constellation, would soon
lose her old name and gain another.

//

One day I will lose my old name and gain another.
It's inevitable. An only child, a girl—
our family name will end with me.
Like dying light, it will fade into night.
If I have a child, I will point
to the sky and trace the constellations—
Orion, Scorpius, Bathala, Granddad—
Connecting dots until all the stars point
to us. When memory fails, I'll build us
into our own new tale, keep the family name
alive if only in the air between my lips
and a listening ear. I know each myth is built
on only fragments of the truth, and eventually,
every myth leads back to God.

Family Story Ending with an Impossible Promise

with a line from RA Villanueva

grandma doesn't dance anymore / her unstable joints / don't allow it / it's hard / to imagine her light / on her feet / hard to imagine my granddad / twirling her like a top / hard to imagine / him at all // pieced together with memories / from others' mouths // if you trace my grandparents back /to the dancehall / where they first met / now you will find a vegan bakeshop / a trendy bar / nestled in the new restaurant row // the past peeking through / the crumbling stonework / if you go back further / you will find a Navy ship / pulled into port / my granddad stepping off // this is where / it all began / at the intersection of Granby / & City Hall Avenue / lit up with the bustle of night // I walk these same streets now / with my own love / & wonder if they walked / this route back then // a door opens & the noise / spills out into the street / a howl piercing / the soft hum of darkness // I'm sure it sounded / much like this / the night they met // the clang of the brass band / the percussion pulling them / to the floor // I try to picture / them together / flushed with the warmth / of new love / as the band played / its final song / & the lights came up / & they walked themselves home // somewhere in this story / is a casket's interruption / a punctuation mark / ending / their imagined forever / when Grandma tells it / she says *when you find love / just pray / you're first to go* // what do I do with such advice / how much of love is just / preemptive grief // I walk down Granby / warmed from a slight buzz / my love's hand guides my waist / as we step into a crosswalk / one my grandparents / may or may not have used / that night / & each night after / when we walk / he grabs my hand / & does not let go / even after we've crossed the street / & this I will cherish / no matter how temporary / just us // walking by what was once / a dancehall / our hands / our skin whispering *swear we will never / not be alive / together*

With Thanks

Unending gratitude and appreciation to Grandma, my parents, and the rest of my family for believing in me as I chased this goal. Thank you for your stories, your support, and your love. The words in these poems would not exist without you.

To Remica Bingham-Risher, thank you for becoming that voice in my head that says "Don't overwrite the ending." Thank you for your notes on craft, for all of our Po-Biz talks, for always having just the right poem to help me figure out what I'm trying to say.

Infinite amounts of gratitude to Dr. Luisa A. Igloria for all of her wisdom, guidance, and encouragement during this process. For making me feel welcome on my first day of class. For helping me to believe in my writing.

To my ODU MFA Po-Hort, thank you for your kind words and helpful criticism, for your careful attention to these early drafts. I value your voices, your thoughts, and most importantly, your friendship. To Nish, specifically, thank you for hyping me up and convincing me to read at that very first open mic during my early weeks in the program. You lit a fire in me and helped me trust my voice, and for that I am endlessly grateful.

To the squad: Lennore Roxas, Ira Patterson, Hunter Greene. Thank you for being my biggest fans. For all the nights we spent procrastinating our work and all the nights we spent paying for it later. For your unconditional love. You are the family I chose, and I will continue to choose you, always.

And to Sean. Thank you for believing in me, especially when I didn't always believe in myself. Thank you for helping me realize I can write poems without always being sad. In any future I can imagine, you are the one constant.

Courtney Tala is a writer from Virginia Beach, VA. She received Bachelor of Science degrees in both Biological Sciences and Psychology from Virginia Tech in 2015. In 2021, she received her M.F.A. in Creative Writing from Old Dominion University. She was the poetry editor for *Barely South Review* from 2019-2021. She is a two-time graduate student winner of the Academy of American Poets College Poetry Prize for 2020 and 2021. Her poetry has been published by *The Academy of American Poets, Glassworks Magazine, Barren Magazine,* and *Constellate Literary Journal.* She is a lover of both science and art, and her poetry attempts to build a space where those two worlds can work together, by using the lyric to interrogate the fixed.

www.ingramcontent.com/pod-product-compliance
Lightning Source LLC
Chambersburg PA
CBHW022124090426
42743CB00008B/998